DRESSING FOR THE WEATHER

Also by Chatter House Press

Banking the Bacon
Essays on the Success of Women
Penny Dunning, editor

Let Them Eat Moon Pie®
The Southern Fried Poetry Slam From 1992 - 2000
by Bill Abbott

Written in the Dish Pit
by Adam Henze

Gems from the Bargain Bin
by Lisa Devon

Warren Avenue
by Nancy Pulley

Where in the World We Meet
by Todd Outcalt

The Mother Poems
A Memoir: The Warrior Queen Novelist and Her Poet Daughter
by Liza Hyatt

Company of Women: New & Selected Poems
Jayne Marek, Lylanne Musselman, & Mary Sexson

Almost Music from Between Places
by Stephen R. Roberts

Some Poems to be Read Out Loud
by Richard Pflum

DRESSING FOR THE WEATHER

Patricia Cupp

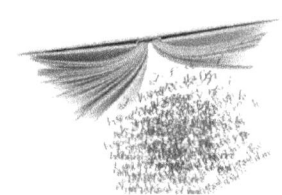

Chatter House Press
Indianapolis, IN

DRESSING FOR THE WEATHER

Copyright© 2014 by Patricia Cupp

Cover Photo by Tonya Cupp

All rights reserved.

Except for brief quotations embodied in critical articles and reviews in newspapers, magazines, radio or television, no part of this book may be reproduced in any form or by any means electronic, mechanical, or by any information storage and retrieval system without written permission from the publisher.

For information:

Chatter House Press
7915 S Emerson Ave, Ste B303
Indianapolis, IN 46237

chatterhousepress.com

ISBN: 978-1-937793-30-2

For my granddaughter Laney,
an amazing work in progress.

ACKNOWLEDGMENTS

"Part of the View" and "First Memory" were originally published in *Rhino*. "Dressing for the Weather" and "Within the Frame" were featured on Poetry on the Buses.

The poems in this collection come from decades of experience, including two years as a Peace Corps volunteer with my husband in Ethiopia. Full marks to friend and fellow poet Tracy Mishkin for helping me select poems and assemble this book. Many thanks to my fellow InterUrban poets and the Writers Center and its community of writers for encouragement to keep at it.

And finally, I am grateful to my family for love and support, and to Mom, who taught me the art of dressing for the weather.

Patricia Cupp

PREFACE

I met Pat Cupp in one of Alice Friman's classes at the Indiana Writers Center. One night Alice asked us to write a secret on a piece of paper, trade with a classmate, and write a poem from our partner's secret. Pat, who has never left behind her time in Ethiopia with the Peace Corps, wrote "Some days, I'd trade my life for a goat." Staring at this sentence with no idea who Pat was, I somehow imagined a former Peace Corps volunteer who misses her days in Ethiopia, about which I knew little more than the name of the capital. Pat and I have been friends ever since, and she has inspired many of my poems, more than anyone else outside my family. There's just something about Pat Cupp.

Pat has been writing seriously since the 1980s. She has published only a few poems, but that's more from modesty than anything else. I love her work, and serving as her editor for this book has been a labor of love. Pat's work is tender and powerful. She has a knack for both political poems and family poems. Like fine wine, her work has bouquet and staying power. I am pleased to share this book with you. I am honored to be her friend.

Tracy Mishkin

Contents

Everything Seems Lacking 3

Knots 4

Shelby Cobra 5

Dressing for the Weather 6

Child in the Barn 7

Walking to Town 8

First Memory 9

No Child Was Injured 10

First Kiss 11

Light in a Vanished Room 12

Circle the Ring 13

The Book of Unwellness 14

Seven Sisters 15

Neighbors 16

Survivor's Guilt 17

Montone 18

Unguided 19

See Naples and Die 20

La Cucina 22

Villa Rustica 23

Savoring the Season 24

Garden of My Aunt 25

Surveying Losses 26

Spirit of the Place 27

Back Road 28

Children of the Queen 29

Naxos 30

Piero della Francesca Made This 31

Part of the View 32

H.D. at Birth 33

To Andrew 34

Requiescat 35

Survivor's Tale 36

Daphne 37

Stone Clean 38

Chemotherapy 39

Threshold 40

Crow Consume 41

Geographic Center of the Conterminous United States 42

The Cram Map Factory 43

Civil War Trail 44

The Emperor's Personal Troops Pass Through Debra Berhan
   on the Day of our First Student Protest, May 1970 45

Debra Berhan, Place of Light 46

Wedding Basket 48

Aleme 49

Moon Reckoning 50

Loss 51

Preferences 52

Tomb of the Hunters 53

Story Problem in Need of Long Division 54

Day After Sixteen 55

Dinner Talk 2005 56

At Tarquinia 57

Waiting Room 58

Testing Ground 59

Park Bench 60

In the Beginning of Cold 61

Ritual 62

The Relocated 63

Photographed Together on the Bridge He Built 64

Within the Frame 65

Notes 67

Everything Seems Lacking

then suddenly
woodpecker
stark against pocked snow
a red cap
white and black bars

he sinks his talons
into suet
strikes deep
tending his hunger
undistracted

Knots

She taught herself to tie a knot.
Now every toy is tethered to another,
bound to chair legs with string,
with ribbons, with scarves.
She is anchored by this new skill
to a world full of knots:
in rugs, in thread, in a swing
hanging from a tree branch.
If you can tie a knot
you have power.

Shelby Cobra [1]

The roadster drawn in childhood,
              its aluminum molded
              by a single crayon stroke,
a fat line from windshield to hood
              to flair of fenders,
              a scoop of door between.
Carroll Shelby remembered
and built that car.

Dressing for the Weather

Black earth and clumps of violets
and one child uprooted
in the mist of first-green wood.
Sweating in a yellow slicker
and mud-sucking boots,
she wades rotten leaves
by a smooth pebbled stream
to the bank's edge.
She balances on a fallen tree,
reaching to bend dark branches lower.
She releases a singular rainfall,
then runs wet and laughing,
full of her own power.

Child in the Barn

She holds the baby chicks, hands curving
to nest. She touches one with her chin,
careful in a way I have never seen before.
In the barn full of animals, the donkey, the lamb,
the calf and the goat, she returns only to the chicks—
this girl of three, who ran to me this morning,
come quick, something has happened,
meaning petals had fallen from the roses.
Her thin shoulder against me, her hair
dark with sweat, she shines in the barn's dust,
this quiet girl who wishes on stars
and is responsible for everything.

Walking to Town [2]

Along the ridge
snow whirls into drifts
across white fields,
peaks on fence posts.
I am ready for this,
my black boots like crows
between the iced furrows.
Tree shadows and my own
the length of the hill.
Finally town without traffic,
only a frozen platform
at West Church and Chestnut,
the mailbox iced over.
On a wall of snow I balance, giant Alice
leaning down to post a letter.

First Memory [3]

At night in the gray room upstairs
after songs and stories,
my fingers in my mouth,
the sheets are close around
and my body is heavy.
On the dresser
white shoes smelling of polish,
outside a branch brushing the screen.
The moon and clouds move
but I am still.
It is warm where my knees touch,
where I coil
between shadow and dream.

Pleasure of the eye looking
at itself with everything around
moving, polished white.
It is only a small risk,
seeing what we were.

No Child Was Injured

The mother's secret,
told years after the war.
Shame at sending her daughter first
into the empty house. Calling her
a brave little soldier like her father
far away. The daughter remembers
hurrying ahead to be first, the thrill
of light summoned by her hand alone.

First Kiss

Some memories need two voices,
my mother and aunt telling the stolen kiss story,
how I sat one day in my frilly dress
on Grandmother's porch, and a little black boy
riding by on his tricycle ran up the steps
and kissed me. So many times told how
he placed his dark hands on my cheeks, how I
lifted my face to his, I think I remember
his hands, damp with summer, his leaning down,
his quick retreat. They say again how white
my dress, that I waved when he looked back.
Mother says my cheeks flushed and I kept
looking down the street that had brought love
rolling to my step in a rush. My aunt said,
the nerve of that boy, and washed my face.

Light in a Vanished Room

It was never clear
why my uncle came to live with us
or why he slept so little.
I watched the light under his door
but I always fell asleep first.
He taught me blackjack,
he went places I knew
were filled with smoke and booze.
He was a veteran of Korea,
a good dancer, lean and quick.
He told me I was a smart kid,
maybe I shouldn't mention the blackjack.
Once with my cousins he sat down,
started playing honky-tonk piano.
He worked two jobs,
hoped to get his family back.
I overheard my aunts talking:
she ran off with that man,
never a thought about him or the girls.
I couldn't imagine anyone leaving him,
a man who skipped stones so easily,
who lived a little dangerously.
It was no effort to love him.

Circle the Ring
Ernesto Neto Exhibit, Indianapolis Museum of Art

you take off your shoes and enter
through the flap of cloth

canvas walls glowing
as if from a day moon
on the other side

what's under your feet
quakes into your head
makes you stampede

drunkenly to the red wave
of sofa then crawl
into the center tent

what's under your knees
tosses you asea
in the ball pit

you've not loved anything
as much as you could

The Book of Unwellness

My sister returns home
twenty-three hours after her surgery.
I help her with the delicate work
of bathing. When she lifts her shirt
I see a drain and a blank, her breast
erased, lymph nodes removed.
The hole will take weeks to close.

Waiting in the office for her exam
my sister meets a patient from Russia
who says women there have no drains,
they carry glass jars under their arms.
This woman wants to save her tubes,
mail them to her Ukrainian sister.

In a dream of my sister's loss,
where her breast has been scooped out
like a melon, an artist paints it back in a swirl
and cups it gently. Then it becomes again
a summer's evening long ago, blue like slate
after a rain. On the sidewalk I am drawing
my little sister round with love. She stands
patiently, one foot on the other, a lily in her hair.

Seven Sisters

what is it among these sisters at her bedside
how no one else may hold this youngest one
who is dying with so little protest

we cousins have watched them for years
how alike they look and sound
their laughter together explosive
Mother says sometimes they become
girls again at the dinner table
bowing their heads before the father
who could not abide their red lips
their private hysteria spilling out
the secrets sisters braid into their hair

and their gifts to one another
not always kind but unstinting
these last three cradling their youngest
whisper to her as they once did
when they watched from the window
arms around each other the storm
approaching how bright they are
together white with lightning flashes

Neighbors

On the porch across the way
my neighbor slumps,
ignoring his lunch tray.
Beside his large wife
he looks deflated.
Their dog barks, a man in hospital white
carries a sack up the sidewalk.
The man turns to his wife
like a question asked.

I wave from my yard but already
they are entering their house
with the man in white.
When these two still
walked the loop of our street
I often hurried indoors
when I saw them coming.

I suffered their homemade wine,
heard a hundred times how they met
in the Navy, World War II. Visits
and revisits to their world map, pins
marking places they had traveled.
At the viewing of their oldest son,
I sat wordless, holding their hands.

I rake the leaves from my yard slowly.
I wait a long time but they do not return.

Survivor's Guilt [4]

Always he tells his story the same:
twenty-two men, banded together,
explorers on a strange island, wondering
at the mountain lions' quiet, the wolves
whose sad eyes follow their passing.
Uneasy they stood before palace gates,
amazed to hear a woman singing, a weaver
chanting back and forth with her loom.

They called to her and she rose to answer,
smiled her goddess smile from the doorway.
But Eurylochus held back at the ushering in,
watched from the window his comrades recline,
lift golden cups to their lips, adoring Circe.

What happened next makes him hesitate still.
Where men once dined, pigs were rooting.
She was laughing, bracelets jangling
as she scattered acorns among them.
The squealing and scrabbling. The way he ran
to find Odysseus, the animals watching him flee.

Montone [5]

Stone hours meted by church bells
the walls skewered with wrought iron
geraniums vining, the swifts diving.
In the piazza old men sitting along the steps
folded around centuries of talk.
Waiters with della Francesca faces breeze by.
Here anyone could wear green robes, sprout rose wings
even the grocer's dog. Everyone in a chorus
of angels about to part the canopy.

Rain that ripens softly in the hills
drums on the wisteria, washes
the streets darker. Shutters
swing open, children call
primo, primo, from the schoolyard below.

Unguided [6]

Rain outside Florence.
How many days since
he's seen someone
he knows.
He can't think
why decay grows
more inviting here.

Sun blistering
in Fiesole.
At the fountain
a paper floats by
just beneath the water.
Don't look he thinks
but grabs the page
caught by a green
sleeve of algae.

She shook her hair in the sun,
smiled and put her hand on his arm
is all he can read.
The penmanship is beautiful.

In the morning
on the train to Padua
he opens the guidebook
where the drifting page
now dried
marks his place.

See Naples and Die
Lacryma Christi ("Tears of Christ") is the name of a celebrated Neapolitan wine produced on the fertile slopes of Mount Vesuvius.

See Rome and die of boredom looking for seven hills.
It's Naples where you find in your bed broken glass
from a cracked light fixture overhead, where trash
spills into fountains, where a visitor to the National Museum
steps over a cigarette butt on the staircase and learns
the world-famous Pompeii collection is touring the U.S.

Exiting the city for Vesuvius, the tour bus
careens around curves, horn honking,
and nearly rams a garbage truck
stopped in the middle of the road.
Workers hoist fallen bags back on the truck,
the driver jabs at the mess with a broom,
indifferent caretaking of one who lives
in the shadow of a dangerous volcano.
The last bag explodes and scatters more garbage
and one animal leg bone onto the road.
Cars and a scooter maneuver by
before the driver finally moves the truck.

You speed on to the guide's recitation of lava flows:
most recent 1944, when ash and rock forced Allies
to evacuate an airbase, and finally what Pliny chronicled,
24 August 79 AD, cloudlike explosion,
ashfall creating the museum's Garden of the Fugitives.
Here even historical daydreams are dark,
victims encased in plaster death throes,
ovens with loaves of bread, an egg in its cup.

At Vesuvius a walking stick and shoe protectors,
rentals for a climb to the rim on a pedestrian pathway
lacking a guard rail, where you read this morning
two sailors yesterday fell to their deaths.
You buy a bottle of Lacryma Christi, sweet spawn of volcanic soil,
and raise your glass to what the Chamber of Commerce promises.

La Cucina

for Barb Shoup, Gari Williams, and Margaret-Love Denman

Sunday in our yellow kitchen,
slicing mushrooms and tomatoes,
ecstasy of garlic and onions,
pine nuts and ripe olives.
From the open window
last night's rain hanging on branches,
beading on pots of basil and rosemary.
We sip wine in a tremble of sunlight.

Villa Rustica [7]

I wake to bread baking golden,
the dog still sleeping on the step.
In and out of shade I follow the road,
turning to each rustling. Higher
where the tree line breaks,
the hills no longer smoke.

In the vineyard by the villa rustica
I'm surprised to see a farmer
who turns his brown coin of a face
to my graveled approach.
Sighting along the perfect order of vines,
we nod at one another, smile at our good fortune
to be nowhere but here early among the grapes.

Savoring the Season

Indiana spring
you clear a few leaves
speared by tips of daffodils
but do not disturb the rest
raking maybe when you see
the raw knuckles of peonies
hardy enough for a late frost

summer weeding
you roll back on your heels
among coneflowers and baby's breath
sweat stinging above your lip
you deadhead and stake and mulch
divide hostas and phlox and lilies
drink from the hose
chew mint

one September morning
you find perfect husks of insects
elaborate cobwebs stretch from plant to tree
you harvest dill and lemon thyme
consider cleaning tools
plant another ornamental grass
sit drinking wine past dark
contemplating heartland bees somewhere
drunk on your African blue basil

Garden of My Aunt [8]

We walk the path, arms linked.
I tell her again these are ferns
transplanted here from her own woods.
We crush lavender between our fingers,
fill our pockets with flower heads.
Only some things have happened.
Lavender is nameless to her,
my identity a puzzle. We are lace
handkerchiefs in a sacheted drawer.

She who taught me plant names:
love lies a bleeding, deadly
nightshade, trout lily. And where
to find bittersweet,
how to make grass whistle.
Under the rose arbor we watch bees
work their singular matter,
her garden free of wilt or rain.

Surveying Losses

The feeding rabbits leave
stubs of pinks in their wake,
hardly a trace of verbena.
Each morning I see them
among the daisies, watching
from the corners of their eyes.
I look them straight on and stomp,
they hop inches, resettle, backs turned.

The garden center recommends
edging flower beds with dried blood.
Sprinkling death's rust,
I circle my garden, imagining
their stopping short, wondering
whose body I have drained.

After enough rain, one is back,
nesting beneath the evergreen.
One day I pull aside the grass,
lift the tufts of fur lining.

Babies sleep, criss-crossing each other
close to their first green taste.
They pulse with newness.
I abandon the blood bath. May the hawk
and cat look elsewhere.

Spirit of the Place [9]

Where our properties meet, my neighbor
and I find something strange in the uncut
grass. A flattened hide. Then a small skull,
a raccoon's. We plant the skull on a stake,
leaving the hide for the rain and sun.

The skull floats above our ghost garden,
rising out of lamb's ear, snowy alyssum,
baby's breath. We show the skull to visitors,
reliving the day we found it, how we first
feared the hair was human. How the sky
viewed through an eye socket
appears profoundly blue.

Back Road

My father and his brothers
grew up in a narrow farmhouse
like the one we drive by now.
Faces in our family album
worn like its faded exterior.

I remember following Grandmother
through woods, stepping carefully,
lichen and sponge bark.
Once I almost touched the foot
of what lay hidden by ferns.

Our car crosses a small bridge,
moves beyond house and woods.
It was a fox. Ants traveling its snout.
I used to dream the fox rose up
after we passed, snorting,

his red tail floating between fronds.
The space where he lay was empty
when I returned in early winter.
I came to think of dying in that way.
We lay among ferns and then were taken.

Grandmother, who feared nothing,
who once killed a rattler with a tree branch,
said that was as good a way as any.

Children of the Queen

The day I purchase the bee repellant I hear there aren't as many this year. No piles of carcasses, just some unoccupied hives. The spray bottle calls the remedy safe for pets and children, claims the breathing of bees (and ground wasps and black flies) is merely disrupted, so they will fly away. The flying away might be forever, bees struck dumb like poor Echo, dissolving. And perhaps there's not enough for bees to eat. Cultivating lot line to lot line leaves no corridor of clover barefoot children must cross carefully. When stunned humans find the last hive empty, we will know the meaning of no more pollination. For now, fewer bees buzzing, less honey. The scent is pleasant as promised.

Naxos

White houses rise to a citadel.
On the spit of land beyond the harbor
a stone door frames the sky,
Apollo's temple, the rest fallen,
luminous in the water below.

Each day we swim the leeward side,
climb together to the ruined sanctuary
to sun ourselves. Evenings
on our balcony we sip wine
and toast the island of the strong door.

Our last day I cross the causeway
to the temple, scale its high foundation.
On the door's threshold, I lean flat
against the frame, sheltered from wind.
Only land, sky, sea.

All afternoon I sit above where the green sea
foams white against black rocks. I watch
wave after wave and feel for the first time
my child move inside, my life made over.

Piero della Francesca Made This

We arrive cool and dry in Monterchi
to see the Madonna del Parto.
Pregnant women once came to the chapel
to pray for an easy birth. In the fresco
twin angels part the brocade curtains of the canopy
to reveal the blessed virgin. We see how the artist,
choosing his mother as model, rendered her
languorous, her garments loosened, her eyelids
drooping. Her hand caresses the swell of her belly
beneath a velvet dress the blue of a low flame.

Part of the View [10]

On far ambas
where purple flowers
ripple to silver among bending grass
piles of stones have names.
In the shadow of the ledge I watch baboons,
the leader lion-maned,
and covet their easy gait
in shrieking raids on farmers' fields.

When I am here,
fists unfolding to palms,
an easy mark for small regrets,
I remember names more easily,
confuse directions less often.

I think of the child
who stops me daily
with the same question:
"Foreigner,
what is the time?"
and I look to the sky.
He circles his wrist with fingers,
brushes the flies and shakes his head,
will ask again tomorrow.

H.D. at Birth

The child travels,
finally, into cold light.
Summoned for an audience
we come nodding and bowing.
We have no words for this.

We want to kiss her head,
blow through the whistle
of her thumb and curling fingers.
Each of us holds her.
Everywhere she looks
our eyes follow.

She rests as a mountain rests,
her bones settling
into a space
everything passes round.

To Andrew

the orchid blooms
watered with ice cubes
here on the window sill
and winter is diminished a little
by magenta, by a gift from my son
whom I first knew as a gift

Requiescat

At fourteen, on display in the choir loft,
I was preoccupied with the girl sitting
one row in front of me, whose substantial
bosom even the flowing robe could not hide.
She wore high heels on impossibly small feet.
I envied her angora sweater sets, her naturally
curling hair, her boyfriend who sent roses.
Her life seemed desire made manifest.

Home again. Another funeral, head bowed,
but the beloved organist isn't there,
just the organ. Hearing the minister read
the familiar passages, green pastures
and anointing, I recall church camp, appearing
as an angel in saddle oxfords to the shepherds
in the fields, the surprise of a French kiss.

For years I carried my white leather Bible to church,
read stories I saw in my View-Master: Daniel
in the Lions' Den, Salome swaying before the king,
the head of John the Baptist. One day I crawled out
of those gold-leaf pages, left it home, opened other books.

Survivor's Tale

Whatever made Odysseus endure
also let him stand in the end
alone, invoking the muse, singing
his failures, his resolve growing
in the wake of remembered suffering.

Imagine the crowd gathering today
at the banquet, giddy for the telling,
pandering to destruction, tallying
victims. Every soldier a hero.
We stare dumbly into the mouth
of loss and declare victory.

Daphne [11]

she runs with no desire
to know her pursuer
a maiden alone in woods
servant of Diana

Apollo it turns out
who follows
matches her stride
closes the distance
she feels his hand at her hair

his breath upon her neck
near the river
almost caught she cries
at the last moment
save me father

then a strange becoming
roots sprouting from her feet
skin toughening to bark
her fingers long and leafing

in this gallery you see her
mouth a circle
in marble so soft and white
it has just cooled

surprise at this stillness of laurel
this price of rescue

Stone Clean [12]

Like Hestia she bides her time,
waves from the window,
seeing them off.
She wants to empty
everything, use it up.
In the kitchen she squints to restore
the architect's blueprints of counters, stainless
rectangle of sink. Her gaze shatters
the window of the oven,
slams shut the pantry door.
Everything flat mounds
under her bottle-glass stare.

Like Hestia she is keeping silent,
raising her adopted children,
meeting with ladies
of the Peacock Society.
She stashes a few valuables,
consults her horoscope.
She sweeps the hearth clean,
dreaming of the day she exits,
asking anything but asylum.

Chemotherapy [13]

I am hacking an exit,
disappearing in a Hopper splash.
Lips opening and closing,
bubbles of sound.
Everything feels on loan.

I reach for my coffee cup and you
are silent. If in this moment
that you are staring at me not speaking,
that I am bringing the cup to my lips,
if we see ourselves clearly
as this man fallen silent watching
this woman who is drinking coffee,
everything might be retrievable.

Threshold

All the world has shrunk to the place you lie curled in sleep's cave. In the deep blue of the night comes a dream of a courtyard, a gypsy leading a mare, dark and flinty. He takes your hand, you think to read the palm. He closes your fingers on the reins, taps his chest. In the light from the open door a moth whirs, digits tumble. You step into the stirrup of his laced fingers. A branch snaps, falls into the lilies. No one wakes. The bow draws taut. Moonlight bright on snow, black holes of animal tracks. You ride reckless toward the sea. The cat rubs against you, your lover sighs. Enough obligation. A digging back into a world disposed to light.

Crow Consume

between the rows
of field stubble
black crows strut
stretching their beaks
toward full ears of corn
silos of it
only a wing away

so immense
people of consume
we slice through skin
use up songs
and prayers
winds and waves rise
dark as bruise

when we hunger
everything burns wild

give us this day
no matter tomorrow
give us this

Geographic Center of the Conterminous United States

Near Red Cloud, Kansas,
blue-white October,
cloud shadows
race across adjacent corn fields
waiting to be made syrup
and cereal. You understand corn
better without machines,
imagine chopping it
with a blade three fingers wide
like the one hanging
in the town hardware.
You hug the atlas against the wind
without math enough to know
what it is this spot marks. Still
the exact center of anything
could prompt a vision,
this belly of land swelling
at the navel, connecting this growing
to every harvest and you
to a nationalism that doesn't suck
the manifest out of destiny.

The Cram Map Factory [14]

maps have
only four colors
and not one ever
borders itself

so difficult finding
common ground

Civil War Trail

At Gettysburg National Military Park
soldiers are buried near where we walk
and monuments—Union square,
Confederate round—tell whose loss,
not forgotten as we forget the garden in winter.

When we stop to examine a row of cannons,
a guide gives us each a lead ball to hold,
asks us to imagine its firing power
across fields of wheat and corn into orchards,
where she points toward some still embedded
in tree trunks. Their impact shattered bone.

We pass the house where the surgeon's boy,
wanting to be of some use besides mopping blood,
gathered amputated limbs, dug a grave,
and covered them, away from the sight
of those next in line.

In the museum we shuffle silently
before photographs of the fallen,
where there was no quiet except
for the ones who lay dead,
so many clutching at their tunics.

In the gift shop we purchase a panoramic postcard,
move toward the bleachers where lights dim
and we look down on a room-sized board,
lights flashing on a diorama and the narrator calling out
the skirmishes by names we gave them later,
tallying the hours, the reversals, the casualties.

We gather outdoors for the pageantry
to marvel at authentic-looking infantry,
to startle at the firing of muskets as they clash,
to watch these who are marching still through a gap in time.

The Emperor's Personal Troops Pass Through Debra Berhan on the Day of our First Student Protest, May 1970 [15]

Afternoon tea at a teachers' college in Ethiopia.
We pause mid-sip to ask, *What's that? Gunfire?*
Only blanks, someone says, *the army on maneuvers again.*
Another teacher bursts in: *Soldiers are shooting at the students!*

I am running up the path from school, soldiers at the gate.
Run home, they order and hold fire, motioning with their weapons.
I stare stupidly at their uniforms. One grabs my sleeve, angry
at my hesitation. The others ignore me, resume shooting
over the low wall. In the distance, the girls run holding hands,
kicking up dust with their flimsy sandals, their faces covered
by white shamas. Bullets sting the stones. Boys clatter rocks
against jeeps, on tin rooftops, and I want them to stop,
see they are outgunned. One falls, comrades lift him
almost without stopping. The road empties.

On the campus of Kent State, noon, a bell ringing,
students passing between classes. Guardsmen
on high ground, combat gear, M-1 rifles.
The girl kneeling, the boy dead before her.
What were they thinking as the soldiers closed in?
So many people said, *If they attended, they were asking for it.*

Debra Berhan, Place of Light

If you can afford to wait, even an egg will grow legs.
                                Ethiopian proverb

The rainy season begins, a clamor on tin
shaking down from above, then pressing in and up.
Sometimes I see one plastic shoe stuck in the mud,
some urgency leaving its owner running on half-shod.

I learn beggars at the gate are never turned away.
I wake to shouting, to donkeys' slow clopping
past our compound on Market Day. Only once
do I ride in a gari. The driver beats the skinny horse,
races another cart, too close. He laughs when it crashes
against us, at my sudden jumping down.

Nothing has a set price and I am no good at bargaining.
Our student coaches me on conventional insult,
urges me to call the vendor thief. At market I stare
at flies crawling over meat. The butcher turns at the sound
I make when the cow, its throat cut, falls to its knees.
At night, I hear bones snapping as hyenas feed.

Most of what happens each day is expected, but not the hills
after the long rains when suddenly a mass of yellow daisies
covers every slope. Meskerem, they tell me, the New Year.
I buy a goat, barter tins for eggs with the neighbor boys,
retread my loafers with tire rubber, plant a garden.
I line doorways with eucalyptus against invasions of ants.
At dusk walking home I see women scattered in a distant field
where they squat, speaking softly to one another,
the circles of their white skirts spread about them.

Days curl into one another long as the Rift Valley
where I look and look without seeing the end of anything.
The cows arrive home, the old one first through the compound gate,
silvery black, her long horns clattering on corrugated metal, then
the rest of the herd. The boy slapping their flanks with a stick.
"Yet abat?" he shouts to each, "Where is your father?"
Later I will understand this means "bastard," as I will learn
the art of greeting, asking after the family, person by person,
and the ritual, no longer tedious, will include me.

Wedding Basket

The bride turns the basket in her hands,
traces the red rim and follows each pattern,
plum, wheat, sea green,
jutting up and circling.
She remembers her mother's fingers
colored as her craft,
reeds following one upon the other
as dreams do in sleep.
She lifts the careful cone
inside whose perfect circle
she lays riches safe for her journey.

Aleme [16]

It is most often late afternoon
when I think of you, Aleme,
as if the low angle of sunlight
is clock and memory.
I am climbing the hill from school to town.
You are hurrying to our chosen place,
toward the ritual of meeting.
You carry your baby brother
wrapped in your shama.
Our walk home is solemn.
When you speak
you tilt your head sideways,
inhaling your words,
your voice a softness
I must lean toward.

Now we are both
women of a certain age,
scrambling less easily
over rock hillsides.
I have a granddaughter.
I think of her like you
whose name means My World.
If we could choose a meeting place,
share again our limited phrases,
would you offer your hand,
could we walk a new path
in your country together?

Moon Reckoning [17]

The fevered infant sleeps,
the machines wakeful.
Glitter of steel at his thin shoulder
when the moon hangs clear of clouds.
In this sterile room she keeps watch.
She must be careful, quiet her own breathing
to listen. Her arms empty, she rocks in rhythm
to a story that will take all night to tell:
      Once upon a time
      in a forest
      moonlit and enchanted
outside this hospital nursery.

Loss

If you write a poem about his death, do not fit it inside a year and month and inside that, a particular day. It is more than the dawn when he passed and you lay down beside him to memorize the way you would no longer fit together. When the sun rises on the anniversary of his death, waking takes the shape of a hand against your cheek, and you remember clearly a night in Venice coming home late on the vaporetto when he pulled you inside his jacket and you leaned back in his arms and everything bright was passing slowly, reflected in the dark water. The drum of the boat's engine that might take you again at midnight on a journey together becomes the rain falling on a garden reluctant to give up its green this December morning.

Preferences

I prefer bare hands and low-burning candles
I prefer simmering sauces, trusting
strangers, anything that requires boots
I prefer the "having been" of an ablative absolute
a boy jumping to touch the doorway's lintel
I prefer the velvet of a goat's mouth
the sting of wood smoke and flower beds without borders
I prefer the word on the page and sitting alone at dusk
when the barn owl comes to hunt
I prefer unlikely encounters and waving again
and again from a distance
I prefer the long way round and keeping a secret
the silence after the deer has fled

Tomb of the Hunters [18]

I want a next world like the one I saw
once in an Etruscan tomb
its fishes and birds in fishfowl space
and us below in boats
smiling and floating far and wide
setting off from this life
to one more aqua

rising on wingfins
every day will sweep
across the valley
to where I rest
in the lace shade of olive leaves
where I brush my lover with sweet grasses
mint upon my tongue
still fortunate among the living

Story Problem in Need of Long Division

At the relief agency they remind us
they can use our donations
not just now in this emergency
but any time. If we should look outside
our neighborhoods to where families
are unsheltered even before the hurricane
or flood or fire, we might cancel the garage sale.
We might fold up the quilt, dust off the rocking chair,
find a lamp to go with it and take them
to the nearest center. We might gather children
onto our laps, read to them about what things
each year can blossom new on old wood.

Day After Sixteen

In the quiet
beyond the dark lantern
think of me
holding you
in the black pocket
kissing each finger
smoothing your hair
reciting all the days' names
known only to us
day of bicycle
day of arrow head
day of arithmetic's secret

my son
do you still hear me
this is the day
after you are sixteen
when you do not ask
for any gift
when you hurry off

are you listening
secrets like bullets
nestle in each chamber
danger unnamed
like days unnamed
breaking us open

Dinner Talk 2005

I could have enjoyed the meal if talk
hadn't strayed from vacations and offspring
to someone saying that crazy thing:
If we're not over there, they're over here.

Over here looking past death tolls,
we shudder at the pump price. We sport
lapel pins and magnetic logos
and drive large. War's nothing but net.
One day soon (I'm guessing here but
I've seen it before) we'll lift our heads
from kissing Old Glory, announce we've sacrificed
just about enough for those people.

I was cornered, white-knuckling my dessert spoon,
my sister giving me that please-not-again look
across the table. But I was seeing craters,
hearing moans, imagining the cities dark.
I couldn't think past the limbless soldiers,
the ones over here. I asked if they knew
any of them. Had seen photographs.
If they ever thought what Iraqi families
discussed when they sat down to dinner.

At Tarquinia [19]

In darkness of a tomb
leopards above the entrance,
the dead awakened
to the creak of ancestral oars.
Gathering their burial goods
they climbed the stairs
toward moonlight.
Did they remember
reclining at banquet,
the flute and pipes,
did they hold up the bronze mirror,
polish its scratched disc
for one imperfect look
before the world
emptied of them?

We who come here centuries later
descend their stone steps,
peer through doorways
into painted rooms finding
only what they did not take.

Waiting Room

No way of settling.
In the half light we cross the lobby
to smoke beneath St. Francis,
count the steps to the gift shop's
beacon of lighted displays.

At dawn nothing begins.
Light slants at the window.
Why remember wake-robin
is another name for trillium.

If we say anything
we only mean make allowance,
let him pass through within the old margin of error.
Or we fear he is dying on the surgeon's table.

We lean into one another like arching trees.
We wish to carry him away from here,
find where lives made over and over
reclaim us without question.

Testing Ground

Evenings she sits covering her eyes,
thinking how to not let death
loom in front of her.
She watches him shivering
beneath a space age silver blanket.

Then comes a favorable report,
like a Book of Hours falling open
to luminous scripture.
Open your eyes, moon man.
More light and light.
She does not know
if she has spoken aloud.

In the hall a cart with a box
labeled soft wrist restraints.
How to believe in a god
whom she can summon
to save one suffering person
above all the others.

Dinner she eats carefully,
resting the fork between each bite.
When it is time to leave she packs
her book, sweater, glasses.
Capable steward shouldering her bag,
she looks back at him, sees
the yellow eyes just beyond the window.

Tomorrow, she whispers,
kisses his forehead, thinking
how she might crawl into his bed,
mold her body the length of him,
how she could merge her strong heart with his,
make the monitor obey her lead.

Park Bench

Carefully he sits,
round shoulders sloping to swollen middle,
relieved to be settled in this safe place.
He does not read or watch
but looks at his chosen spot
with eyes made blue marbles by cataracts.
His slow hands smooth worn flannel,
then rest easy in the cradle of his thighs.
His face wears the vacancy
of a patient waiting.
He draws his shoulders back
and gives himself to sitting.

In the Beginning of Cold [20]

Sometimes thin circles of ice
swirl on the surface
just before the pond freezes.
The final morning with my father
I saw what later I called his spirit.
In the light from the open door
it lifted from his body,
a brown moth guided safely
from the house. I turned
and looked into the distance
as he had, for days,
taking the measure of things.
He had only said,
"I can't tell just yet.
You can't tell right away."

Ritual

After the service for your uncle
we walk together to the grave site.
You read aloud names on the tombstones,
your boyhood edged by this churchyard,
your father's grave a few rows away.
Under the white canopy we look out
where fields roll toward Big Sugar Creek.
My ashes should be scattered there, you say.

Having eaten the mourners' meal,
we linger over smaller matters,
close together under the trees.
The children appear quietly
bearing small tin cups
balanced on a red flowered tray
they have found in the church nursery.
We lift the cups to our lips,
sip and nod, accept another.
Tireless hosts and guests.

A passing pickup truck spills music,
slowing at the fresh grave's canopy.
Our shy stewards offer clover chains.
Further out where grasses sprout seeds
the curling bark of the birch
glows in the setting sun.

The grave fills with our aching,
empties a little with glad memories.
Bees float in the fountain.
We make our way back.

The Relocated

It is a long corridor
gray carpet and rose draperies
a door opening to the oval room

in greeting my sister
a moment's faltering sense
how farfetched all this is
what may open beneath our feet

weight of stone on the rim
away from light and rain
we among the living cover
but not forever as we think

underground in Paris I once saw
what became of graves exhumed
the bones arranged in tunnels
with no guide we followed Boy Scouts
flashlights illuminating passageways
lined with skulls, crossed arm and leg bones

we walked the folds of corridors
guided by stacks of the relocated
heard the living paralleling
our passage on the other side

we exited quietly into sunlight
from where so many lay together
their bones yellowed ivory
polished one after another

my father's casket is closed
destined for a mausoleum
in the Court of the Apostles
his bones will never
keep company with others

Photographed Together on the Bridge He Built [21]

It is my father's hands I remember
a workman with trowel
breathing even with the labor
the scoop and slap of mortar
his grunt with lifting blocks
stair stepping a foundation
flooring and framing
sawdust in his dark hair
the rhythm of roofing
three strikes to the nail

it is his level I use
when I kneel to eye
the next landscape timber
and any time I need a tool
or wear blisters using one
because I have removed my gloves
it is my father's prompting
his pleasure in strength
his hand firm upon mine
as it is in the photograph taken
in autumn on the bridge
he built long ago

Within the Frame

You cannot feel the air
shimmering between these leaves,
the water slightly faded on the canvas edge.
Even if you wait the flowers
will not fold and colors drain to black.
This lesson in seeing allows
only light's erosion, follows you
from the gallery to your garden.
This year you settle on
the longest bloom of daisies.
Each time you weed you touch
the flower centers and rub the yellow dust
between your fingers and dig
at the plot's edge a few more inches
for next year's larger plan.

Notes

1. *Shelby Cobra*
   In a class with Jared Carter, we were challenged to write a poem about a car. I remembered seeing a Shelby Cobra at an auto show with my husband Michael. It looked like a car a child would draw—a gorgeous racing green color.

2. *Walking to Town*
   A ski weekend in Michigan, where I am, once again, dressed for the weather.

3. *First Memory*
   This poem originated in my first "clustering" writing exercise, based on *Writing the Natural Way* by Gabriele Lusser Rico. I read a draft to my mother, who told me how she polished my shoes and washed my shoelaces every night when I was a toddler.

4. *Survivor's Guilt*
   The witch Circe turned almost all of Odysseus's men into pigs. Eurylochus was the only one to escape and warn Odysseus.

5. *Montone*
   When Barb Shoup received funding to rent a villa in Montone, she invited Gari Williams, Margaret-Love Denman, and me to join her for a writing retreat.

6. *Unguided*
   Michael traveled to Italy alone one summer on a grant. This poem is based on his journal, with some added fictional elements.

7. *Villa Rustica*
   A poem written after walking outside Montone in early morning. The smoke on the hills is a mist called *sfumata*.

8. *Garden of My Aunt*
   A collage of several people I have known, remembered as an elderly aunt.

9. *Spirit of the Place*
   My neighbor Annie Aldrich and I started a ghost garden after viewing the Georgia O'Keeffe exhibit at the Eiteljorg Museum. When we discovered a skull on our property line, we dubbed it our *genius loci*, Latin for spirit of the place.

10. *Part of the View*
    I didn't need a watch in Ethiopia. The boy in this poem was disgusted with me for not wearing one, as if I weren't a bona fide foreigner.

11. *Daphne*
    Apollo and Daphne is a 17th century statue by Bernini, who depicted the Greek myth of the god Apollo pursuing the nymph Daphne—until she begs her father to save her. He can only turn her into a tree, a transformation that the artist captured in marble.

12. *Stone Clean*
    Thinking of women who raise other people's children and never marry reminded me of the Greek goddess of the hearth, Hestia.

13. *Chemotherapy*
    An Edward Hopper painting came to mind as I wrote about Michael's chemotherapy, how it exhausted us both. As difficult as it is now, this treatment was brutal in its early days. He suffered it with grace, in silence.

14. *The Cram Map Factory*
    Michael and Barb once took their Learning Unlimited students on a field trip to the George F. Cram Company map factory in Indianapolis.

15. *The Emperor's Personal Troops Pass Through Debra Berhan on the Day of our First Student Demonstration, May 1970*
    We learned of the tragedy at Kent State through the news shortly after a similar event took place at our teacher training college in Ethiopia. The girls were always fiercest in the student demonstrations. They shouted about unity and threw rocks onto tin roofs, making a tremendous noise. The boys joined in behind them. This put the girls out front in relative safety when the soldiers began shooting. The boys were hemmed in by the stone walls of the houses that lined the street.

16. *Aleme*
    Aleme was the nine-year-old daughter of our housekeeper in Debra Berhan and a surrogate daughter to me.

17. *Moon Reckoning*
    When Steve Shoup had a bad motorcycle accident, I stayed with Barb at Loyola Hospital in Chicago. During our vigil, I once mistakenly pressed the elevator button for the pediatric floor, and when the doors opened, they opened onto suffering.

18. *Tomb of the Hunters*
    The Etruscans were a pre-Roman culture on the Italian peninsula. A fresco on a tomb in Tarquinia depicts people in a boat with fish above them and birds above the fish. Drawn lacking perspective, the fresco seems to represent flying fish.

19. *At Tarquinia*
    There are approximately 100 tombs at Tarquinia. The authorities open each tomb for only an hour at a time to maintain appropriate humidity levels, so visitors don't know which one will be open when they arrive.

20. *In the Beginning of Cold*
    During my father's final illness, my friend Danny Koehler convinced me to go home for a weekend sooner rather than later.

21. *Photographed Together on the Bridge He Built*
My father, Joe Shull, owned a construction business. Growing up with a talented father, I thought all men could build things. When my parents lived in Plainfield in the 1980s, they had a wooded lot with a creek. My father built a bridge over the creek, and I bought him a plaque for the bridge that said, "We are known by what we build."

www.ingramcontent.com/pod-product-compliance
Lightning Source LLC
Chambersburg PA
CBHW060214050426
42446CB00013B/3069